BETWEEN LAKES

ALSO BY JEFFREY HARRISON

The Singing Underneath
Signs of Arrival
Feeding the Fire
The Names of Things: New and Selected Poems
Incomplete Knowledge
Into Daylight

Between Lakes

Jeffrey Harrison

Four Way Books
Tribeca

For my father,
Robert Sattler Harrison
(1931-2012)

"But today
It is my father who keeps stumbling
Behind me, and will not go away."
    —Seamus Heaney, "Follower"

*

And in memory of Mark Lanier,
(1958-2019)

"While I walk on
the moon keeps pace beside me:
friend in the water."
    —Masahide, 1723

Library of Congress Cataloging-in-Publication Data

Names: Harrison, Jeffrey, author.
Title: Between lakes / Jeffrey Harrison.
Description: New York : Four Way Books, 2020. |
Identifiers: LCCN 2019054770 | ISBN 9781945588532 (trade paperback)
Subjects: LCGFT: Poetry.
Classification: LCC PS3558.A67133 B48 2020 | DDC 811/.54--dc23
LC record available at https://lccn.loc.gov/2019054770

This book is manufactured in the United States of America and printed on
acid-free paper.

Four Way Books is a not-for-profit literary press. We are grateful for the assistance we
receive from individual donors, public arts agencies, and private foundations.

This publication is made possible with public funds from the
New York State Council on the Arts, a state agency.

We are a proud member of the Community of Literary Magazines and Presses.

CONTENTS

EKTACHROME DAYS

The way it turned everything blue
even bluer

like the north wind
on days like today

deepening the lake
to cobalt

and bringing fall
a little closer—

an old slide found
in a desk drawer

held up to the light,
moving the past

into the present,
into a day

too blue to last.

1.

VARNISHING DAYS

These days between late spring
and early summer are like paintings
already hanging but not yet finished
the week before the Summer Exhibition
(once the custom at the Royal Academy),
still waiting for their final touches
and smelling of linseed and turpentine:

everything fresh, the paint still wet,
the taut sky primed with a wash of blue.
The Siberian irises, not yet
unfurling, their buds still tight,
look like paintbrushes saturated
with ultramarine; buttercups
spatter the meadow with yellow.

From an arbor of scribbled vines,
blossom-clusters of wisteria
dangle, glistening with last night's rain.
A wood thrush calls in liquid trills
from deep within the background's
mass of pale, soft greens. The air
chills while the sun warms the scene.

May these days remain unfinished
a while longer, with no artist
jostling his way in
to apply some final flourish
or a coat of varnish that will
only darken. Let the bumblebee
fumble among the blossoms.

GLAZING A WINDOW

As usual, when I begin
I feel as though I don't
know what I'm doing
and have to learn it all
over again, and sure enough
on my very first pane

the size and shape of a page,
the blade of the putty knife
pulls the ribbon of soft
glazing compound right
off the strip of trim I'm
trying to press it into.

I start again, and then
again, and eventually
get into a rhythm, making
small adjustments as I go
and taking pleasure in
the way the knife blade

compresses the putty
into a smooth bevel
while its sharp edge cuts
a clean line against the glass,

the excess curling away;
and I move from pane

to pane, still making
mistakes, of course, but
emending them as best
I can while trying not
to lose my focus, trying
to get into a groove

and stay there. And when
I'm done, I wipe away
my smudged fingerprints
so my labor doesn't show
and the window glistens
with the day's reflection.

NAÏVE ROOFSCAPE

(*Aix-en-Provence*)

Beyond the French doors leading out
to this fourth-floor rental's balcony, open sky
above a pre-Cubist arrangement of
ochre walls, blue-gray shutters both open
and closed, and terra cotta roofs—all studded
with innumerable accessories and doodads:
small chimneys gathered in familial groups
and wearing metal caps, a Celtic cross
and two stone urns atop the church;
a gold ball below a flag-like weathervane
at the apex of a pyramidal tower,
the pointy, floppy tops of three cypresses
projecting up like elf hats; satellite dishes,
the skeletal metal wings of TV antennas,
and, best of all, the shiny cylindrical
vents whose tops, spinning like pinwheels,
flash festively with sunlight—all these
conduits and valves and instruments
that in one way or another mediate
between worlds, between a sky saturated
with sunlight and the streets below, noisy
with the cries of children on their way to school
and the clang of workers in blue jumpsuits
assembling scaffolding against the wall
opposite, keeping it all from falling apart.

MUSHROOMING

Christopher and Helen, our new expatriate friends,
meet us at their favorite winery
where they fill their plastic jerry cans from hoses
exactly like the ones at gas stations,
as though they're planning to go back home to Aix
and treat their lawnmower to a nice red.
Instead, they take us in their forest green Peugeot
to the home of their old friend Brigitte
in a village at the foot of Mont Ventoux—
actually, not a village, Brigitte corrects me,
but "*un hameau*," a hamlet. The French
are exacting about such distinctions, though Brigitte
has a kind, mischievous smile. Back in the car,
we tear along a series of rutted, stony roads
that web the mountainside, with Brigitte
directing Christopher, "*à droite, à gauche, encore à gauche*,"
until we come to a grove of pines, cedars, and oaks,
where she says the mushrooms are hidden.
We fan out under the trees, searching the slope,
while Brigitte, looking elfin in her orange hoodie,
waves a stick like a wand, pokes at the dried pine needles
or the dead leaves under wild boxwood bushes,
and sings, "I think there are some over here,"
like a mother leading her toddlers toward Easter eggs.
We laugh and follow after her, cutting the stems

with a tarnished knife she lends us, warning
"*Faites attention*," because the blade is sharp.
And gradually we fill our plastic shopping bags
with gnarled orange caps, stained green,
which, much later, back in the States, I learn
are called *Lactarius deliciosus* or
orange-latex milky, like a shade of paint,
the field guide commenting "edible, although
not as good as the name *deliciosus* suggests"—
but we already suspect that (they look awful),
and we'll later unload most of ours on
Christopher and Helen who clearly think of them
as a delicacy . . . but right now we're
just hunting for them among the sunspots
on the forest floor, filling our bags,
and calling through the trees, the whole afternoon
gathering into the giddy moment
that Brigitte keeps calling us back to.

ELIZABETH BISHOP AND THE GRATEFUL DEAD

(San Francisco, 1968-69)

Whether she ever saw them perform we don't know,
but she did go to a Janis Joplin show,
and Thom Gunn's account of smoking a joint with her
backstage at a group reading makes it easier
to imagine her chatting with Jerry during a break
(about Billie Holiday, or Baudelaire, or Blake)
if not dancing in the aisles during one of the band's
already notoriously labyrinthine jams,
like the one between "Dark Star" and "Saint Stephen"
(a new song in their repertoire that season).
He would have been twenty-six, she fifty-seven.
She might have let it drop that Donovan
wanted to record "The Burglar of Babylon,"
he might have praised her trippy "Riverman,"
but she probably wouldn't have uttered the phrase
she'd used in one of her unfinished essays
to describe the music of a rock band she'd seen
several times that year: a fucking machine—
though that might have led to a flurry of wit
or perhaps a killer rendition of "Love Light,"
with Pigpen lewdly rapping, in the second set.
Unlikely? Still, I'd like to think it happened—
my favorite poet meeting my favorite band.
Her partner then was in her twenties and
had connections to the music scene. Also,

in the year and a half she lived in San Francisco,
the Dead gave over sixty-five performances
so you'd think she'd have seen them once. Is
that too much of a stretch? Well, this just in:
five or so years later, on one of her trips up
to her beloved Nova Scotia, Bishop
brought as a present for her teenage cousin
a copy of *Europe '72*—a triple album
gathered from live concerts—telling him
the Grateful Dead was a band to know about . . .
and also that it was okay to smoke pot.

SHARING A PAINTING

("Madonna and Child with Two Angels,"
Piero della Francesca)

For half an hour we had the painting
mostly to ourselves,
and the longer we stood there
taking it in together,
the more the people drifting
around us seemed to disappear.

We spoke quietly
when we spoke at all,
as though trying not to discomfort
the Mother and Child, though they
seemed imperturbable,
inhabiting a world apart,

along with the two angels
who stood behind them on either side,
vigilant, looking in different
directions, like (I said)
celestial Secret Service agents.
The one in the blue robe, head globed

as though in a space helmet,
fixed us in his gaze and seemed
to be guarding a back room
that you said looked inviting,

illuminated by a slanting beam
of tangible sunlight.

I couldn't help remarking
that the basket of gauze cloth
behind the other angel
looked like a pie topped with meringue
placed on an upper shelf to cool,
beyond the reach of mortals.

We marveled at the tenderness
of Mary's delicate fingers
cradling the feet of the Child,
who appeared to weigh
several pounds less
than if he'd been part of our world.

He shared his mother's
pensive serenity,
had the face of an old man
he would never live to be,
and wore a coral pendant
like a branching artery.

He held his right hand up
as if to call for silence.
But we were done with talking.
It was just the two of us
and the four of them
in that unearthly stillness.

LOST PHOTOGRAPH

I wish I knew what happened to the photograph
of my father and me that my younger brother took
when we were in our twenties, maybe
still in college, home for Thanksgiving.
We were helping our father cut firewood,
a ritual since we were boys, though back then
we didn't do much more than tag along.

Maybe Dad and I were already out in the woods,
and Jeremy was catching up,
listening for the chainsaw to find us.
Maybe we were gathering the logs
and loading them into the back of the Jeep
as he approached with his camera,
thinking he'd surprise us—

but Dad and I spontaneously turned
and in unison gave him the finger
with our hands encumbered by work gloves
just at the instant he snapped the shutter.
My brother printed the photo and gave it to me,
a black-and-white five-by-seven—
too big for an album, and never framed.

I haven't seen that photograph in years.
I've looked for it but can't find it anywhere.
Maybe some day I'll open a book
and it will fall out, surprising me once more
in the way it catches my father and me
united in a moment of buffoonery,
our smiles showing through our phony glares.

THE LIGHT IN THE MARSH GRASS

was alive: small creatures aglow and crawling
one after the other down each tall green blade—
thousands of them bending at all angles—
along the quaggy edge of the salt marsh cove
the three of us had paddled our kayaks into . . .

luminous bits of green-gold sliding down
the myriad stalks, but inside them, as if the marsh
were sucking down the warm light through
innumerable living straws, drop after drop
in a wavering, steady, mesmerizing rhythm,

and for once no explanation we could think of
(that unseen ripples on the cove's mirrory stillness
focused the late sunlight in eely ribbons
that scrolled down the blades of spartina)
could diminish the marvel we had chanced upon,

and we gave up trying to explain it, gave ourselves
to it—as if we had ingested some hallucinogen
that opened our eyes to what was there all along
but had gone unnoticed, each of us in our own pod
of selfhood floating on the fetid, primordial cove

now held together in awed suspension by these grasses
aswarm with lights that also flowed in waves through us,
wanting it not to stop, asking ourselves why
we'd never seen what had been going on for eons,
asking how we could keep it, knowing we could not.

BEACH GLASS

"Absent one, how I miss you on this shore
that conjures you and fades . . . "
—Eugenio Montale

A wall topped with shards of broken bottles
runs along the lane that winds up the hill
to this house above the Ligurian Sea
not far from where the great poet lived.
One of his lizards visits my balcony.
And that mysterious "you" of his,

during my time here, has become *you*.
I've looked for you among the lemon trees,
in waves flashing through canopies of pines,
in upper windows fluttering with sheets,
and on a small beach below rocky cliffs,
its gray stones crisscrossed with white lines.

And there I found these tiny, glinting beads
of colored glass hidden among the pebbles—
most in shades of green, but some amber
like drops of honey, and some between, the color
of your eyes, and two or three the pale blue
of inlets where foam has clouded the water.

GIRL CARRYING A SUITCASE

("New York, ca. 1960," Garry Winogrand)

Younger in the photo
    than my daughter is now—
        eighteen or nineteen,

the same age as my wife
    when I first met her—
        she would now be not quite

old enough to be my mother,
    more like an older cousin
        I saw only in summer

and would steal glimpses of
    or find ways to be near . . .
        just as I kept circling back

to this girl's photograph
    at the exhibition
        to study again

the way her body bends
    slightly to the right
        to offset the weight

of her fabric-covered suitcase
    against the lighter raffia bag
        in her other hand;

the tapered cut
    of her sleeveless dress
        printed with black-eyed Susans

(one centered over a breast);
    and the way her silver bracelets
        gather at her wrists

below the almost-dimples
    on the inside of her elbows,
        the photo's shadowed foci.

And since bringing home
    the postcard I bought
        at the museum shop,

I've been searching her image
    like a figure recovered
        from my own past,

someone I almost recognize,
   though her head
      is veiled in glare,

and her hair coming loose
   from her braids conceals
      the right side of her face.

She gazes downward,
   toward the sidewalk she
      has just stepped onto

from the busy crosswalk,
   unhurried and alone
      amid the crowd

of the city she is either
   leaving or returning to
      but not arriving in

for the first time
   (she is too unguarded),
      lost in herself,

thinking perhaps of whoever
    she has just been staying with
        or is about to visit,

someone who—whether cousin,
    friend, parent, or lover—
        must surely adore her.

If only I could find her
    and show her this photograph
        which, almost certainly,

she has never seen,
    since it was printed for the first time
        only recently,

decades after
    the photographer's death . . .
        or at least send her this postcard

I've been keeping on my desk
    these last few weeks,
        giving this stolen

glimpse of her past
  back to her, so she too
    might be taken

by this young woman
  who was once herself,
    like someone held dear

who left long ago
  then one late afternoon
    shows up at the door.

2.

LAOCOÖN

is what I've named the wisteria
growing at the back of the house,
its thick vines twisting like serpents
around the invisible figure
I imagine struggling as in the famous
sculpture at the Vatican.

Or maybe I'm the figure, grappling
to cut the tentacles back
so they don't engulf the house,
my two children having escaped
by growing up and moving away,
while I've been left behind to battle

this writhing monster of a plant
sent by some god as punishment
for a crime that's different in each version
of the story and no one, including me,
remembers for sure, though I know
I must be guilty, I always feel guilty.

BREAKFAST POEM

Those rare mornings when our father made breakfast,
the eggs tasted different—they tasted better,
because he liked to fry them in butter
sunny side up, instead of over easy
in bacon grease, which wasn't bad either,
only the usual, so not a novelty.
And we didn't care about the lack of bacon
(for that our father didn't have the patience).
We still had toast, though not with margarine
but, again, with butter that our father spread
imperfectly, in little flavorful chunks.
And we had those eggs, whose orange yolks
looked up brightly from our blue-glazed plates
as if to greet the day, the way he greeted it,
exclaiming, as he finally sat down with us,
"Isn't this the best breakfast you've ever had?"

THE SAME FATHER

Looking back on it now, it seems hard to believe
that on the nights he put us to bed
I could lay my head against his chest
as he read to us, without thinking about how,
the next morning, he'd come into our room
and pull the sheets back to see if they were wet,
and if they weren't he'd give us a reward—
like something (though I didn't think of it then)
out of the story he was reading, whose words
I listened to with one ear, while with the other
I focused on the unfamiliar drone
resonating inside him, drawing me in.
The reward was just an ordinary dime, but he
called it a "diamond," like something precious
from the tale I found harder to follow
as I gave myself to that mesmerizing voice
beyond words, alien but comforting,
almost Gregorian, yet somehow belonging
to the same father who, morning after morning,
bestowed the glinting prize on my younger brother
with a bright voice, before turning to me
and flinging back my sheets to expose
the sour odor of my worthlessness.

MAKING MONEY

When I asked my father what he did at work,
he said, "Make money," which I took literally.
But when he took me to his office one day,
I didn't see much evidence

besides the adding machine on his desk
with a roll of paper running through it
about the width of a dollar bill. Was that
how he made the money?

He let me play with it, and I liked pushing
the plastic buttons, and especially
pulling the lever that made a sound
like a cash register—

but no drawer full of money popped open.
In another part of the building he took me to,
pianos were being made—big curved pieces,
the screech of saws,

wood scraps and sawdust all over the floor,
the smell of wood and glue. I liked best
the funny little hammers covered in felt
and got to take one home.

But what did pianos have to do with money?
My father explained he was a businessman
and said it was like playing a game.
Like Monopoly, I thought,

with its colored bills. My mother didn't believe
money was real. "It's only paper," she'd say,
and sometimes she acted like we didn't have much,
which annoyed my father,

who, after all, spent his whole week making it.
Money was a mystery, it was hard to figure out,
like a piano's insides—all those moving parts
somehow adding up to music.

C STUDENT

"The world should be run by C students,"
my father liked to say. He especially liked
to say it to me, because I always got A's.

He, of course, always got C's, a fact
he cited with self-deprecating pride
as though it were the firmest possible proof

of one's good character . . . whereas getting A's
meant you were a show-off, or a pantywaist,
or (worst of all) an intellectual.

So, while other fathers were lecturing their sons
for "not living up to their potential,"
I was being mocked, because, in his book,

getting A's was a mark against me, my own
Scarlet Letter, worn invisibly on my chest
with a strange combination of pride and shame.

Sometimes I threw it back in his face:
"Maybe I don't want to run the world."
"No," I can still hear him say, "you want

to stand on the sidelines and criticize it."
Fair enough, but even after I grew up
and found my way, he never stopped saying

"The world should be run by C students,"
and I never doubted it was directed at me,
though I did begin to wonder if he was right:

he didn't run the world, but he ran
a company, whereas I (as he might say)
have never run a damn thing in my life.

HIGHER EDUCATION

Antioch, Berkeley, and Columbia
were the ABC's of colleges
my father said he wouldn't pay for—
breeding grounds for radicalism
he called them, as if their campuses
were giant petri dishes spawning
toxic cultures. Our own pathology
was pretty toxic at the time, both of us
stubbornly refusing to learn
anything about each other, or
about ourselves for that matter, stuck
in a rudimentary pattern of
defining ourselves as opposites.
I wouldn't even look at Kenyon,
his beloved alma mater, despite
its long tradition as a school for
future poets. I hadn't read a word
of Robert Lowell or James Wright yet,
but I'd read Ginsberg, and the first stop
on my college tour was Columbia,
and that's where I ended up going.
And my father, to his credit, must
have seen it was the right place for me
or at least was unavoidable,
so he let me go, and he paid for it.

And the only price I had to pay
was, when I was home on holidays,
to suffer his barbed commentary
about the very education he
was financing, which ironically
had to do with the core values of
Western Civilization. I can't
remember—is forgiveness one of them?
We both got a C in Forgiveness
but later bumped it up to a B minus
when, in a surprising twist, my son
ended up at Kenyon. My father
took real pleasure in that, though he
was already dying by then. I thought
of him at graduation, how proud
he would have been for his grandson
who, he might have joked, was a better
student than he had ever been—all
our ignorance put aside at least
for that one day of celebration.

KITCHEN INCIDENT

Only now, after decades, even after his death,
is the smoke finally clearing from that room
where I was kneeling on the brick hearth
making a fire—something, after all,
that my father had taught me how to do—
when he walked in from work, in a business suit,
to find the kitchen filling up with smoke
because I'd forgotten to open the flue.

And not until now have I bothered to consider
what might have happened at the office that day
or whether it was simply his frustration
at ceaselessly battling his acerbic teenage son
that led him to say, "You don't know how to do
anything right," then shoulder me out of the way
as he crouched down and reached his blue-sleeved arm
above the flames to find the damper's latch.

At long last, I wish I hadn't told him
to shut up, and can let go of my indignation
at the way he lunged for me, grabbed me by the arm,
and tried to spank me as if I were a child,
only managing a glancing blow as I pulled free
and made for the door, not looking back
until now to see him standing there
bewildered and alone in that smoke-clogged room.

MASH

Not the TV show, with its laugh track
effervescing in the background, but the movie
starring Donald Sutherland and Elliott Gould
and directed by Robert Altman. My father
loved that movie so much he loaded us up
in his panther-like black Thunderbird
and drove us to a far-flung drive-in
when we were only ten, twelve, and fourteen—
like some essential male initiation
carried out on all three sons at once.
And we loved it, all those shenanigans
that made war seem fun, despite the gore,
which hardly fazed us anyway since we
were seeing the same thing every week
in photos coming out of Vietnam.
And the sex, well, we knew *something*
about that too, much of it wrong—
there was a lot in the film we didn't get.

Not long after that, I found my father's
high school yearbook in the attic and brought it
downstairs, then pointed to his classmates, asking
which were his friends and where they were now.
I was shocked to hear that some had died
in Korea. He'd failed the army physical

after injuring his knee playing football.
Now I wonder if he felt guilty, or left out,
though he wasn't one to dwell on such things.
He liked action. He liked *Patton*, which came out
the same year as *MASH*, and once said Truman
should have let MacArthur invade China.
But more than anything he liked to have fun,
playing touch football with us or driving around
in his 1946 Army Jeep, doing chores
or giving us rides around the woods and fields.
He loved to imitate Hawkeye's whistle of surprise
but never got the intonation quite right.

Decades later, after he retired, I gave him
the video and, later still, the DVD,
which we watched together during his last year.
He didn't laugh as much but seemed to enjoy it,
though between the chemo and the disease
I'm not sure he was getting everything.
The theme song about suicide meant
something different to me now, but I don't know
if he thought about that, or about the grim
initiation he and I had gone through
when we cleared out my brother's apartment
(no whistling like Hawkeye then).

He'd never gone to the movies to think,
and what's wrong with that? He never knew
who Robert Altman was or considered that *MASH*
was as much about Vietnam as Korea—
or if he did, he didn't care. It was just
a damn good funny movie, and that was plenty.

HOW IT WORKED

It was hard to sit there with my father,
watching one of my sister's girls playing
a set of tennis against my son or daughter,
because he'd forget himself and with a groan
of disappointment or a grunt
of sympathetic exertion make it clear
that he was rooting for my sister's child
and against mine. There was no use
calling him on it, because he'd deny it
and get angry. So I would get angry
but try not to show it, until I couldn't
stand it any longer and would get up
and walk away. That was how it worked
between us, the unspoken building up
like thunderheads above the tennis court,
while the kids played on, not caring who won
and hardly noticing the sky had darkened.

SHOOTING A SLINGSHOT WITH MY FATHER

It still hangs there, the old frying pan
he tied to one end of a length of clothesline,
knotting a heavy iron hook to the other end
before flinging it up into a giant hemlock
(its lowest branch too high to reach) until it
caught, and the pan swung there, a perfect target
we could shoot at with a slingshot
from the cabin's porch at cocktail hour
or while he was grilling a steak.

When you hit the pan, it would ring out
like a bell over the lake, and echo back,
and then you'd have to wait for it
to stop spinning before shooting again—
either that, or time your next shot perfectly,
which he could do, and I could do sometimes.
"Don't sight it," he'd say. "Keep both eyes open"—
advice that could have been about life,
though unlike me, he didn't think
in metaphors, but called things what they were.

None of us had better aim than he did—
he'd honed it growing up in the boonies
with no one his age to play with—
though I gave him a run for his money.

It was one competition between us
that never got nasty. And in his last year,
when the tumor robbed him of his aim
and made him suddenly old, he liked to sit
on the porch and watch me shoot, laughing
with quiet pleasure each time I hit the pan,
as though he were the one making it ring.

3.

DEAD TREE

Twenty feet into the woods
and visible from the kitchen window,
it has grown simpler each year
almost without my noticing

and now resembles a tree
drawn by a small child
before the leaves have been added
(but there will be no leaves),

its skeletal crown reduced
to four main limbs
that abruptly end
at a few blunt branches,

with no smaller branches
angling off them.
It's like the way we forget
the dead, slowly,

almost without noticing,
the details of their personalities
falling away
until we have trouble recalling

their gestures, intonations,
humorous remarks,
even the faces
of those we loved,

reducing each of them
often to a single trait
("Granny was depressed,"
"Uncle Lou was a prankster"),

like a jagged stump
enshrouded in ferns
below the absent, once-
breathtaking canopy.

VINES

For years he'd been tenacious about cutting them,
so it was startling, when I visited, to see
the way he'd let the vines infest the trees
around the house: climbing euonymus
insinuating itself into the treetops
and extending false branches out into sunlight.
At some point he must have just given up.

So, for three days, during his midday nap,
I ventured out and cut them with an ax
where they clung thickest to the trunks of maples,
ashes, walnuts, locusts, splotched sycamores,
and the giant, dying cherry out back,
and watched the foliage that had invaded the crowns
go limp and die. And then I pulled them down.

It felt good to be killing something
that was so unequivocally a metaphor
for the invasive life form trying to kill him—
winter creeper, a type of bittersweet,
though there was nothing sweet about it,
and later I read that cutting it back only caused it
to spread underground, and surface somewhere else.

THE CRUELTY OF METAPHOR

It was not because he was frightening or vicious
that we called him "the shark" but because he
always had to keep moving, always be
doing something, like mowing through swells
of tall grass on his tractor or sinking the hooked teeth
of his chainsaw into a locust. We used the nickname
mostly with affection, and he was proud of it.

So it felt all the more cruel when he got sick
and spent each day on the glassed-in porch,
listless on the sofa as if washed up
onto a fake reef in a giant aquarium,
vacantly eying, on the other side of the glass,
the cardinals, finches, and red-winged blackbirds
that darted around the feeder like tropical fish.

GRATITUDE

My father and I got along best
during his last year and a half
when he had cancer. Saying that
feels wrong: one cannot be grateful
for a brain tumor. And I would never
have wished on him the way his life
was diminished to sitting on the sofa
watching either TV or the birds
coming and going from the feeder.

And yet the mild brain damage
that showed up as a cloud on the MRI
had the unexpected effect of
smoothing away the sharp edges
of irritability, impatience,
and competitiveness. No more
sarcastic remarks. No resentment.
Maybe some unspoken bewilderment,
but mostly, to my surprise, gratitude.

Sometimes I wanted him to get angry—
at the disease, at his bad luck,
even at me. Instead, he thanked me
for refilling the feeder, for clipping
his toenails and soaking his swollen feet

in warm water. He thanked my mother
for the soups she made, for the smoothies
that soothed his infected throat.
He even thanked me for reading him poems.

And so, despite the decade or more
the cancer stole, I'm grateful for
that year and a half, for those two springs
when we watched the goldfinches turn
from green to yellow, like autumn leaves,
for the flame-emblazoned shoulders
of the red-wing, and for that new,
gentle father who kept telling me
how grateful he was that I was there.

LAST ADVICE

The night before my father died
I dreamed he was back home,
and I in my old room
on the third floor, and he
was calling up to me
from the bottom of the stairs
some advice I couldn't hear
or recall the next day when,
standing over him
back in the ICU
full of the chirping of machines
we had decided to unplug,
I remembered the dream
and heard him call my name.

LAST LOOK

We thought we were ready
until the technician removed
the breathing tube—
and he opened his eyes.

The head nurse assured us
it was just reflex:
he wasn't seeing anything,
wasn't really even there.

Still, it looked as though
our father had woken up,
not that he was going to sleep
for the last time—

his opaque stare
and thick breathing
a rebuke
I can't escape.

WAITING WITH CYNTHIA

While my brother and I
waited for our father to die,
one of the hospital's chaplains
came in to visit us.

Her name was Cynthia,
and the first thing she did
was read some passages from
The Book of Common Prayer—

but she stumbled over
every other line.
Then she read some different prayers
and did just fine.

Afterwards, she explained
that she was a Baptist
and the Episcopal prayers
felt cold and strange. She asked us

if there was anything else
we wanted her to read,
and I said the Twenty-Third Psalm,
though I knew it might lead

to tears. Maybe I wanted
to cry, to prove I wasn't
some stiff Episcopalian
for whom emotion was alien.

She asked what our father was like,
and we tried to tell her
while he was lying there
utterly unlike himself,

his eyes not seeing anything,
his breathing labored
without the ventilator.
"What was your favorite thing

to do with him?" she asked.
Right away, one of us said
cutting firewood
and the other agreed.

"What was his favorite song?"
That stumped us. It felt wrong
that we didn't know,
until we recalled how,

back in the days
when he drove us to school
he used to sing the songs
from Gilbert and Sullivan plays.

Then Darren, the young minister
from our parents' church, came in
and my brother whispered,
"Here comes the competition."

That made Cynthia laugh.
It was like something Dad would say.
Darren, in a very formal way
but without stumbling at all,

read some prayers that had
too many references to evil,
as though our father were in need of
an exorcism before he died.

After he left, I told Cynthia
what Dad had said about Darren:
"He's too religious."
That made her laugh again,

but she said he meant well.
We realized gradually,
that she was planning to stay
for as long as we needed

which turned out to be
four or five hours—
to the very end, and then
beyond the end, because

she wanted to spare us
the ordeal of having to see
our father's body being
zipped into a plastic bag.

Meanwhile, she kept us company.
We talked about a lot of things—
our children, her son
who lived . . . in Kansas City?

I can't remember much of it.
It felt strange to be chatting
about this and that,
as if nothing was wrong

and our father wasn't there,
but then we'd turn back to him
and fall silent again,
and that also felt strange.

Nothing about it felt right,
but Cynthia helped us through.
Our father would have liked her,
if he hadn't been the one dying.

DEPARTURE

What we thought was his last breath
wasn't. His last breath came
maybe thirty seconds later.
Then my brother and I waited
for the doctor on duty
to come in and make it official.

It shouldn't have surprised me
that the doctor was a woman,
but it did—and even more
that she was young, and beautiful,
her big, kind, dark brown eyes
not yet hardened by her profession.

She said she was going to give our father
his "final exam," which made it sound
like a test in school.
She busied herself around him,
then filled out some forms,
recording the time of death.

It was confusing to be
distracted by her beauty
just when we were crossing into
the vast country of Fatherlessness,

as if we were abandoning him
as soon as he left us.

She lingered a moment to ask
if we needed anything else,
holding us once more
with those eyes, so deep and alive.
I finally said no,
thinking, *Don't go, don't go.*

POLITICS OF THE DEAD

1.

When we opened his "Bye-bye File,"
we found, among the bank codes,
passwords, insurance information,
power of attorney, and living will,
a dozen or so right-wing
articles our father had snipped out
of newspapers and interspersed
among his final instructions,
as if even in death he needed to get
the last word in. We took them out
as we paged through the documents,
shaking our heads in disbelief
and making a little pile. "What do we do
with these?" I asked when we were done.
"That's up to you," my brother said, then:
"It's obvious he meant them for you."

2.

It's true, he used to send me articles
like that, and I would send them back,
with all the clichés and abuses of language
circled and annotated in the margins.

But years ago I asked him to stop,
then outlawed politics as a topic
of conversation, since what we did
was not so much converse as
bark feral outbursts. We kept
the subject buried as best we could,
like an underground cable.
But here were these articles again,
as if he meant to undermine
my grief for him. I didn't read them,
and when no one was around
slipped them into the recycling bin.

    3.

Those last few months, I almost hoped
he would snap at me: it would have meant
he was getting better. He never did.
Instead, he watched Fox News,
which was sad since it was all he could do—
though why not, say, the Tennis Channel?
It was as if that indoctrination
was somehow necessary
before entering the next world,
which you'd think would be beyond
politics, beyond the reach of all

those snarling dogmatists that sent
the rest of us fleeing to the kitchen,
where my mother cried and I
tried not to listen, tried to hold
my tongue, and sometimes did.

4.

I don't know where we were,
but my father was sitting across from me
talking politics—though not yet
with any venom. Still, I was afraid
that at any moment he might blurt
one of the remarks that made me
unable to breathe, much less speak,
like I'd bitten into an electric fence.
And to prevent that, I said,
"I can't believe you want to keep
this argument going even after
you're dead." Then, as I lay there
awake in my bed, I realized that,
because the dream was mine, I
was the one who hadn't let it go—
and from here on, it was mine alone.

FATHER'S DAY

My first father-
less Father's Day came
a little too soon
after the funeral,

plus my wife and kids
were out of town,
depriving me of
my own father-

hood, and rendering
me temporarily
wifeless. When I
called my mother,

she wasn't home:
*Please leave a
message*, said
my father's voice.

MY FATHER'S SWEATER

I'd almost forgotten about
　　the Norwegian sweater
　　　　I "borrowed" from my father

when I was in college
　　and wore so often
　　　　that its intricate design

of grayish, creamy checks
　　inside a navy grid
　　　　flecked with a lighter blue

became so much a part of me
　　that even he began
　　　　reluctantly to think of it

as mine. Later, I sewed
　　patches made from socks
　　　　inside the fraying neck.

I never gave it back,
　　but over several decades—
　　　　as the patches came loose,

one of the elbows gave out,
    and a cuff unraveled—
        began to wear it less.

What a shock to find that sweater
    in an old footlocker
        at the bottom of his closet

the week after my father died,
    its pattern as familiar
        as it was unexpected.

When had he stolen it back—
    and why, since now it looked
        too threadbare to be worn?

It felt like a game
    he had won posthumously,
        and I didn't mind

that the joke was on me,
    only that the game was over.
        Now it would always be

my father's sweater.
    What could I do but,
        trying not to rip it further,

take it from the trunk,
    slip my arms through the sleeves,
        and pull it over my head?

4.

BETWEEN LAKES

I used to sneak off with a folding chair
down the hill, some evenings, to the edge
of the inlet between lakes, and just sit there.

It was so quiet I could hear the distant grinding
of tiny creatures boring inside the trunks
of the spruces next to me, though sometimes

the kingfisher flew by, chattering to himself.
I'd try to get caught up in the nets of late sunlight
that wavered over the trees on the other bank

or lose myself in their green-gold reflections
shimmering on the inlet's fluid mirror.
Eventually, I'd hear someone ask, "Where's Jeff?"

and someone else answer, "I don't know."
How quickly I revealed my whereabouts
by calling to them, or just climbing the hill,

depended on my mood, the beauty of the evening,
and something else harder to pin down.
But it was never right away. I lingered in

that watery, mutable, in-between zone,
the sky deepening with the possibility
that I could be both there and gone.

SCENE FROM A PHOTOGRAPH IN A DREAM

What was I doing in my childhood room again?
And why, on my old bed by the window,
was there a snapshot of my brothers and me
in our late teens, wearing blue jeans and sweatshirts,
contentedly napping in the living room?

My younger brother was lying on the sofa,
while below him, on the carpet,
my older brother and I lay next to each other.
What took me by surprise was
the way one of my hands was resting

on my brother's chest with a natural,
unselfconscious intimacy, as though
there were no secrets between us,
and without the slightest awkwardness
that might have caused me to move my hand away

if we had woken up. Only sleeping
in a living room within a photograph
inside a bedroom in a dream—
never when I was awake and he was alive—
have I touched my brother with such tenderness.

YARD WORK

My father owned sixty acres of land
that he worked on every weekend;
whenever I go out to work in my own yard's
modest plot, I think of him.
While I sit on the mower cutting the lawn,
he's on his Massey Ferguson tractor
bush-hogging a field, and I remember how,
as a boy, I rode on his lap,
bouncing up there above the world
in the wordlessness of the engine's roar.

When I'm repairing a board on the shed
or sawing a limb off a tree, balancing
on a ladder, he's nearby.
Yesterday, replacing the mailbox post
the snowplow had knocked over,
I thought of the time we tried to dig a rock
out of the driveway, only to discover
that—like our feelings about each other?—
nine-tenths of it was below the surface,
and it wasn't going to budge.

Just so, the base of the broken post
was stuck in the ground and wouldn't come loose
no matter how much I dug around it

or pried with a crowbar.
Then my wife came out and suggested
hitting the post-end with an ax
and, with the blade firmly planted,
lifting it out. On the third try it came free,
revealing a square recess of concrete
I could slip the new post into.

That small compartment under the earth
reminded me of the one we'd placed
my father's ashes in. I had to reach
way down there and, with my bare hand,
scoop out the dirt that had fallen in,
breathing in the dank underground air.
And when I looked up and said to my wife,
"It takes two people for a task like this,
even if one of them is just giving advice,"
it was his voice coming out of my mouth.

OXBOW

Strange that I feel his presence
more at the lake than in Ohio
where he spent most of the year,
as if the membrane between worlds
were more porous here.

As I wade in to take my first swim,
he's looking down from the porch,
about to ask me how the water is—
obscured from view, when I look up,
by sunlight slanting across the screen.

It's been over a year since he died,
but I'm dreaming about him again:
sitting at the dinner table with us,
he tries to make a point but can't get
the words out through his inflamed throat.

We walk to the river to have a picnic
and only then realize we've chosen
his favorite spot, an oxbow
where the current slows and the water
deepens before the sharp bend.

THINNING THE SPRUCES

I've become ruthless with the spruces
that crowd the hillside between the cabins and the lake,
filling every available space and leaving no room
for the slower growing maples and birches.
I yank the little ones up by the roots
and get down on my knees to cut
the trunks of the larger ones with a handsaw.
Soon I'm covered with sweat, needles, and dirt,
and my wrists, between my cuffs and work gloves,
are flecked with blood. Anyone watching me
might think I hate the spruces, but I don't.
They look cheerful, and I like the way,
after a storm, raindrops hang from the tips
of their bristly fingers. Now the cut trees lie
scattered over the hillside, like fallen soldiers.
I begin to gather them up in great armfuls,
as many as I can hold, then carry them awkwardly
into the woods, and throw them down the gully.
I am stumbling with one of these unwieldy bundles,
hugging its prickly green mass to my chest
as if I were in love with it, when I hear

my father thank me. I heave the load
over the edge, and pause to think. *Am I*
still trying to please him, even in death?

I don't know the answer, and keep going,
thinking, *Would that necessarily be a bad thing?*
and: *This needs to be done, and I'm doing it.*
"You have to do it every year," he told me
last summer, his last one here. I answer now,
"I know. Otherwise they'll take over."
"—take over the world," I hear him echo,
sounding a little paranoid, but I know he's joking.
"The Green Menace," I say. "They've infiltrated
the ecosystem and must be rooted out!"
After a pause, he says, "They breed like rabbits,"
and I point out that now we're mixing metaphors.
And the conversation goes on in my head
as I keep working through the afternoon,
unable to stop myself (the same way he
did chores), sweating, my heart pounding,
struggling with the bundles, hugging them
then heaving them into the gully.

ROCKING CHAIR

The rocking chair
   on the dock
      rocks

on its own,
   unoccupied,
      back

and forth
   on the bleached
      boards

between the lake's
   wave-streaked
      blue

and the sky afloat
   with fat white
      clouds,

its fading layers
   of slate-blue
      paint

cracked and flaking
   like ancient
      lichen,

worn in places
   to the weathered
      bone . . .

back and forth
   of its own
      accord,

or propelled by
   an invisible
      force

that seems to be more
   than just the
      wind,

as if someone were
   sitting there,
      back

from the dead
    for an after-
        noon,

staying only until
    the wind itself
        dies.

DOUBLE VISITATION

There I was with my father again alive
walking around the back yard together,
and I hardly noticed that it wasn't our back yard
or that he looked like he was in his fifties.
We were laughing at something, joking around,
each comment making us laugh even harder.
But then he was crying and I didn't know why,
his face contorted, unable to speak. I turned
and hugged him and whispered in his ear
the words I wanted to say and he wanted to hear . . .

and as if I had uttered some magic formula
I found myself sitting in a movie theater
beside my suddenly alive again brother.
The movie ended, and as the credits rolled,
we both agreed that it was good. Then I said,
"But I think I fell asleep for part of it,"
and started telling him the dream I'd had,
how our father had visited from the dead,
and what I'd done—and, to show him, did again,
whispering those same words to my brother.

AMONG FLOWERING MILKWEED

What drew us first to the stand of roadside milkweed
was its fragrance pollinating the early dusk,
so sweet we wanted to breathe it in, make it part
of ourselves, and almost thought, as we approached,
that we could hear as well as smell it—a faint,
low whir—before we made out in the dimming light
what we took at first for a swarm of hummingbirds
probing the rosy globes, darting from one
to another, then holding still midair, their wings
ablur. What they were, we realized, were sphinx moths,
drinking the nectar in through tiny filaments.
We took it all in too, for those few drawn-out moments,
almost hovering ourselves among the milkweed,
holding still at the edge of the gravel road.

MORNING ROW

I push my mother out for her morning row,
and she maneuvers her guideboat so the bow points
toward the other end of the lake, and then begins,
one oar creaking in rhythm and both dripping
as she lifts them out of the water for each stroke,
but those sounds grow fainter as she gets farther away
until, leaving the bay and entering the greater lake,
she's entirely beyond earshot, the sky
a blue dome of silence enclosing the lake,
though her oars still keep the rhythm visually,
sunlight flashing off their wet blades like a signal.

She rows down the lake's mile length, past boathouses
whose owners have changed more than once
since she was a girl, but she still knows them by the old names—
Jones, Palmer, Turnbull, Maurice, Snow—
as if she were rowing into the past, and she thinks perhaps
of the summers she spent here with her maiden aunt
and the English boy who came over during the War.
Now she is getting smaller, passing the point
tufted with watergrass halfway down the lake,
until she becomes a light speck moving along the far shore
before disappearing altogether under the mountain.

She is still adjusting to life without my father
who just two years ago would have been the one
waiting on the dock to pull her up. She was here
when he sent the almost daily letters
of awkward courtship I found bundled in the attic.
Now, six decades of marriage ended, she's here
without him again, writing him letters that can't be sent
and I'm not going to read, except maybe after . . .
and just as I begin to imagine life without her,
she comes back into view, small as a water strider,
her white hair like a handkerchief against the lake's blue.

And as she moves slowly closer, zigzagging a little,
I remember how she's always claimed that my birth
in mid-October was the easiest of her four children
because she'd spent all summer up here rowing
and was in fabulous shape when she went into labor.
Now it's inconceivable that I somehow came out of
her small body—but, of course, I did, and soon
was brought up here, and a few years later I was
learning to row in an Adirondack guideboat
just like the one she's coming toward me in,
its varnished body glowing in sunlight.

I remember splashing the water with the oars
and bashing my knuckles because the handles crossed
and you needed to put one hand over the other—
and there was always the danger of crashing
into something, since one of the principles of rowing
is not being able to see where you're going.
My mother called instructions from the dock
as I call to her now—"left oar" and "right oar"—
then pull the boat up the slip and sit on the bow,
keeping it steady as she climbs out,
taking her hand until she finds her balance.

ALL DOWN THE LAKE

It wasn't so much that the dinner conversation
had bored me as that I was simply tired
of words, particularly my own. So afterwards
I slipped away and followed the path down
to the boathouse, where I sat in a lawn chair.
The lake was perfectly still, the inky hills
on the far shore mirrored between two skies
of deepening blue and streaked with clouds
tinged with the last pink. At first I didn't notice
the strange sounds, then didn't recognize them
as human: the faint, distorted, jumbled voices
of dinner conversations all down the lake's
mile length, sliding across the glossy surface
only to rebound off the shore and swirl together
in a confusion of murmurous babble.
Now and then a weird inflection or wild laugh
broke free from the hubbub and twisted up
like a bottle rocket left over from the Fourth.
It was a relief and, really, a pleasure
not to make out the words, or even the coherent
intonations of sense-making and just focus
on the hallucinatory, far-off din. Then slowly,
as the dinner parties one-by-one dispersed,
the voices dropped away until only
a few remained—less alien-sounding now—

then none, the lake itself a mind
that had finally quieted its chatter
just as the first stars glimmered into being
and a bullfrog started calling, deep and steady.

ACKNOWLEDGMENTS

Many thanks to the editors and staff of the following publications in which these poems first appeared, sometimes in slightly different form:
32 Poems, The Academy of American Poets (Poem-A-Day series, Poets.org), AGNI, The Cincinnati Review, Five Points, The Gettysburg Review, The Hopkins Review, The Hudson Review, Image, The Kenyon Review, Manhattan Review, Miramar, The New Republic, Pleiades, Plume, Poetry Northwest, Salamander, The Southern Review, Southwest Review, Terrain.org, upstreet, Woven Tale Press, and The Yale Review.

*

"Higher Education" also appeared in Best American Poetry 2017, edited by Natasha Trethewey, with series editor David Lehman (Scribner, 2017).

"Double Visitation" also appeared in Pushcart Prize XLIV: Best of the Small Presses (2020), edited by Bill Henderson.

"How it Worked" also appeared in American Life in Poetry, a syndicated newspaper and online column edited by Ted Kooser and sponsored by the Poetry Foundation.

"All Down the Lake," "Glazing a Window," and "Varnishing Days" also appeared on Poetry Daily (poems.com).

*

Grazie di cuore to the Bogliasco Foundation for a residency
during which some of these poems were written, revised, or
begun.

Heartfelt thanks to friends who helped me shape these
poems and this book: first and foremost Robert Cording, and
including Karen Chase, Chard deNiord, Keith Dunlap,
Alan Feldman, Jessica Greenbaum, David Henry,
Edward Hirsch, Sara London, Carol Moldaw, Lewis Robinson,
Peter Schmitt, Bill Wenthe, and Charlie Worthen; to
Martha Rhodes and everyone at Four Way; and to Julie,
William, and Eliza Harrison, the cardinal points of my
compass.

*

"Ektachrome Days" is for David Shapiro.
"Varnishing Days" is for Bob Cording.
"Mushrooming" is for Christopher Carsten and Helen
    Steenhuis.
"Elizabeth Bishop and the Grateful Dead" is for Peter Schmitt.
"Lost Photograph" is for Jeremy Harrison.
"The Light in the Marsh Grass" is for Charlie and Jock
    Worthen.
"Beach Glass" is for Julie.
"Sharing a Painting" is for Eric Karpeles.
"Waiting with Cynthia" is for Cynthia Holloway.

"Thinning the Spruces" is for Karen Chase.
"Rocking Chair" is for Marylynn Gentry, in memory.
"Morning Row" is for Anne W. Harrison.
"All Down the Lake" is for Jessica Greenbaum.

Jeffrey Harrison is the author of six previous books of poetry: *The Singing Underneath*, selected by James Merrill for the National Poetry Series in 1987; *Signs of Arrival*; *Feeding the Fire*, winner of the Sheila Motton Award from the New England Poetry Club in 2002; *The Names of Things*, a volume of selected early poems; *Incomplete Knowledge*, runner-up for the Poets' Prize in 2008; and *Into Daylight*, winner of the Dorset Prize, and selected by the Massachusetts Center for the Book as a Must-Read Book for 2015. He has received fellowships from the Guggenheim Foundation, the National Endowment for the Arts, and the Bogliasco Foundation, among other honors. His poems have appeared widely in magazines and journals, as well as in *Best American Poetry*, *The Pushcart Prize: Best of the Small Presses, Poets of the New Century, The Twentieth Century in Poetry*, and other anthologies, and been featured regularly on *The Writer's Almanac, American Life in Poetry, Poetry Daily*, and other online or media venues. He lives in Massachusetts.

Publication of this book was made possible by grants and donations. We are also grateful to those individuals who participated in our 2019 Build a Book Program. They are:

Anonymous (14), Sally Ball, Vincent Bell, Jan Bender-Zanoni, Laurel Blossom, Adam Bohannon, Lee Briccetti, Jane Martha Brox, Anthony Cappo, Carla & Steven Carlson, Andrea Cohen, Janet S. Crossen, Marjorie Deninger, Patrick Donnelly, Charles Douthat, Morgan Driscoll, Lynn Emanuel, Blas Falconer, Monica Ferrell, Joan Fishbein, Jennifer Franklin, Sarah Freligh, Helen Fremont & Donna Thagard, Ryan George, Panio Gianopoulos, Lauri Grossman, Julia Guez, Naomi Guttman & Jonathan Mead, Steven Haas, Bill & Cam Hardy, Lori Hauser, Bill Holgate, Deming Holleran, Piotr Holysz, Nathaniel Hutner, Elizabeth Jackson, Rebecca Kaiser Gibson, Dorothy Tapper Goldman, Voki Kalfayan, David Lee, Howard Levy, Owen Lewis, Jennifer Litt, Sara London & Dean Albarelli, David Long, Ralph & Mary Ann Lowen, Jacquelyn Malone, Fred Marchant, Donna Masini, Louise Mathias, Catherine McArthur, Nathan McClain, Richard McCormick, Kamilah Aisha Moon, James Moore, Beth Morris, John Murillo & Nicole Sealey, Kimberly Nunes, Rebecca Okrent, Jill Pearlman, Marcia & Chris Pelletiere, Maya Pindyck, Megan Pinto, Barbara Preminger, Kevin Prufer, Martha Rhodes, Paula Rhodes, Silvia Rosales, Linda Safyan, Peter & Jill Schireson, Jason Schneiderman, Roni & Richard Schotter, Jane Scovell, Andrew Seligsohn & Martina Anderson, Soraya Shalforoosh, Julie A. Sheehan, James Snyder & Krista Fragos, Alice St. Claire-Long, Megan Staffel, Marjorie & Lew Tesser, Boris Thomas, Pauline Uchmanowicz, Connie Voisine, Martha Webster & Robert Fuentes, Calvin Wei, Bill Wenthe, Allison Benis White, Michelle Whittaker, Rachel Wolff, and Anton Yakovlev.